Dd

Bela Davis

Abdo
THE ALPHABET
Kids

abdopublishing.com

Published by Abdo Kids, a division of ABDO, PO Box 398166, Minneapolis, Minnesota 55439.
Copyright © 2017 by Abdo Consulting Group, Inc. International copyrights reserved in all countries.
No part of this book may be reproduced in any form without written permission from the publisher.

Printed in the United States of America, North Mankato, Minnesota.

102016
012017

 THIS BOOK CONTAINS
RECYCLED MATERIALS

Photo Credits: iStock, Shutterstock

Production Contributors: Teddy Borth, Jennie Forsberg, Grace Hansen

Design Contributors: Christina Doffing, Candice Keimig, Dorothy Toth

Publisher's Cataloging in Publication Data

Names: Davis, Bela, author.

Title: Dd / by Bela Davis.

Description: Minneapolis, Minnesota : Abdo Kids, 2017 | Series: The alphabet |
    Includes bibliographical references and index.

Identifiers: LCCN 2016943884 | ISBN 9781680808803 (lib. bdg.) |
    ISBN 9781680795905 (ebook) | ISBN 9781680796575 (Read-to-me ebook)

Subjects: LCSH: English language--Alphabet--Juvenile literature. | Alphabet
    books--Juvenile literature.

Classification: DDC 421/.1--dc23

LC record available at http://lccn.loc.gov/2016943884

Table of Contents

Dd

Dan has fun with **dad**.

Dd

Don **d**raws a picture.

Dd

Daisy **d**igs in the **d**irt.

Dd

Danna plays with her **d**og.

Dd

Diana **d**oes a **cheer**.

13

Dd

Drew **d**ives on the sli**d**e.

Dd

Dakota **adores d**ancing.

Dd

Dave **d**rives his car.

Dd

What **d**oes **D**elilah play?

(**d**ress-up)

More **Dd** Words

dinosaur

dragon

door

duck

Glossary

adore
to like very much.

cheer
a special chant used by
cheerleaders to excite the crowd
or team at sports games.

Index

abdokids.com

Use this code to log on to abdokids.com and access crafts, games, videos, and more!

Abdo Kids Code:
TDK8803